The Phoenix Living Poets

———❦❦❦❦❦———

ON THIS ATHENIAN HILL

The Phoenix Living Poets

★

ON THIS
ATHENIAN HILL

by

JENNIFER COUROUCLI

CHATTO AND WINDUS

———————

THE HOGARTH PRESS

1969

Published by
Chatto and Windus Ltd
with The Hogarth Press Ltd
42 William IV Street
London WC2

★

Clarke, Irwin and Co Ltd
Toronto

Printed in Great Britain by
William Lewis (Printers) Limited
Cardiff

Contents

To my father

That balding Celt, my father, knows
the exile of the bone
divorced from landscapes bred in one
as water subdues stone.
While I, who married into Greece,
no banishment can find
but, rather, an extension of
the country in my mind.
I walk the marble hills of Greece,
and he his limestone rock,
and wonder how his Irish blood
will out in Hellene stock.
I longed for beauty as a girl
and how I used to stare
into my glass, expecting it
to grasp me by the hair.
Habit dies hard but now beyond
the shadow in the glass
I see my daughters' substance and
know beauty came to pass.
One daughter has Minoan eyes
set in Athena's head,
the other, struck in drachma,
would raise Alexander dead.
My father sets his blessing on
what Celt and Greek devised;
the marble of the Parthenon
is limestone crystallized.

On this Athenian hill,
islanded in air,
pull the green growth of pines
above the last roof, the stair
that climbs red earth to rock,
you'd see the whole thing spin
concentric like a top.
It's possible within
this orbit not to know
the limits one has set
oneself. The mind may leap
on truth and hold it, get
to grips with God — for God
is light and here the light
is palpable. It fills
one's mouth with gold, one's sight
is solid with it, one's
whole self becomes a cup,
pressed down and running over,
for God to reckon up.
Or, if you do not own
to God, forget the word
and bring that noble beast,
your body, here. A bird
would fly it in a day
or so, an angel in
an instant. You, without
belief, must trust to skin
and bone, hoist in a metal
box. But, say you're here
(I'll wait your miracle)
grounded in Greece, I swear

your elements would change
burned in the Attic light —
not change but crystallize
to what is definite.
The Lykabetos hill
pierces the city's crust;
stand on the marble rock
and know you're made of dust,
a mote in the eye of God,
or atom spun in space,
informed with intellect
receptive to His grace.
I tell you, in that light
there is a further plane
of meaning. Size is seized
and emptied. Things contain
essential shape, not relative
but self complete.
I've seen a leaf of cyclamen
enlarge to meet
my sky. I've picked a blade
of winter grass and crammed
incalculable time
into a moment, dammed
the flood of being down
to a drop of dew and drunk.
If you should hold your arms
around a cypress trunk
and look along its height
you feel yourself become
an arrow aimed by God.
That term again! there's some
compulsion here that makes

all definitions dumb
without its reference.
Well then, the Greeks ferment
their grapes with resin, here
the pines release a scent
that permeates the air
and fills the lungs as wine
a glass. One can't escape
the alchemy. The mine
where lead is turned to gold
is dug and found the stone
the wise men sought. You need
a certain space alone
on this Athenian hill
to leap on truth. I write
my own experience,
renascent with the light.

The statue of Poseidon, National Museum, Athens.

Perfection stuns the senses — that
dynamic Poseidon
who hurls his missing trident at
one's head, explodes upon
the retina like fire. One feels
as if the bones consume
their marrow, as though blood congeals
to bronze, that limbs assume
a patina and hollow eyes
are ringed with verdigris.
Before the tongue solidifies
to clapping brass there is
a lurch — imagination slips
into the sea. Deep down,
spreadeagled, taste with metal lips
fierce salt and stiffly drown.

Two thousand years the eyeballs stare
up through a glaze of green.
The seaweed drags the rigid hair,
the sand sifts inbetween
a crust of shells and fluted flowers.
The weighted form subsides;
soft mouths of fish, a billion hours,
the liquid tug of tides.
Forgotten. Lost. Abruptly — shock,
steel cables biting in,
contraction of the spawning rock,
torn from the womb and spin
unwieldy, working, jerking, burst
the barrier and break
the massive water, surface, thirst

11

for sight of sun and take
the choking air again.

I stand,
emptied of self and find
that Poseidon has come to land
constituent in my mind.

Pheidias

They say that Pheidias
sailed near the wind. He made
his marble Gods of human
clay and disobeyed
tradition. Certain well —
known faces, it was said,
recalled Apollo's profile
or Athena's head.
This smacked of hubris but
was difficult to prove.
The Opposition saw
its chance and made a move
to get at Pericles
through Pheidias. They sued
the man who compassed in
his mind all magnitude
of form; whose careful hand,
sustained by brittle bone,
mastered the infinite
and let out God in stone.
They charged this working man,
who cut them down to size,
(wiping the sweat and dust
out of his sun-filled eyes)
with theft of public funds
and clapped him into jail.
Pallas Athena's gold,
down to her fingernail,
was found exact while in
the reaches outside time
an Archimedes shouted
to be born. The crime

recoiled on the accusers.
Pheidias gave up
the ghost while they survived
to mix the hemlock cup .
for Socrates.
                    "Crito,
do not forget the cock
for Asclepios."
                    It crowed
when Christ stood in the dock.

Ulysses deduces the world is round

I can't believe that those
old, seafaring men,
sailing beyond the rim
of each horizon when
the earth was reckoned flat
were ever taken in.
Constantinople fell
before the world could spin
and let Pythagoras
and Aristotle out
into the cloisters, where
they barely raised a shout
to launch Columbus. Yet,
don't tell me Ulysses
was such a fool to think
he'd flounder down the brink
of the earth's boundaries,
homing to Ithaca?
That wily Greek observed
through ten corrosive years
where sea and heaven curved
and took his bearings. He
was conversant with stars
and saw them hurtle down,
swinging between the spars
of ships to dip beneath
the taut horizon. He
discounted this, aware
of islands endlessly
dropping behind — quite sunk
the Cyclops, Circe sunk —
and Ulysses alone,

with sea and heaven drunk
roaring around his head.
There never was a man
with such a will to live,
producing plan on plan
to stay alive. He must
have reckoned with the lurch
of latitude, made sums
from stars and, in his search
for constancy, deduced
the world was round. He made
his harbour long before
those Captains, mad for trade,
Columbus, Drake, da Gama,
set their course, before
Magellan beat the Horn.
Pirate, Conquistador,
trader in space and slaves,
founder of colonies —
I can't believe that they
knew more than Ulysses.

The City

I've heard them speak about the City
till I know the streets,
the churches on the corners and
a certain house with sheets
hung on the balcony to air.
I always see it so
which means it must be morning. Later
there would be a row
of flower pots, spilling scarlet petals,
and a cat, composed,
exchanging topaz signals with the sun.

    The house is closed,
perhaps torn down, a modern block
erected on its bones.
What's that to me? I am the heir
to more than sticks and stones.
I know of other houses, built
before the Turk had set
his foot inside the door. Their loss
has been my gain. My debt
is to the City which has piled
riches on riches, crammed
into my mind. I am the lake
for which the stream was dammed.

The walls still stand in places. For
a thousand years they kept
the pass between the East and West
impregnable, except
when crossed Crusaders turned their cannon
there. (Leaving their wives

cooped up in Northern castles where
they chafed away their lives
until some likely lad turned locksmith.)
Sick of the Holy Wars,
goat's flesh and painted boys, the Franks
stormed through the City's doors
and stayed for fifty years. The Turk
came last.
        We have become
familiar with Islam. It
has been the medium
through which we had to breathe or die.
Some choked on it but still,
enough survived.
        There was a yard
behind the house until
the family left; flagstoned, with pots
of basil and a tree
of bitter oranges beside
a cistern. I can see
the place and smell the stink of mouldy
stone mixed with the sweat
of fear. They rammed their furniture
below the parapet
and bundled down the children one
by one. The mother crawled
in last, clumsy with petticoats,
clutching the baby, shawled
shackled to her breast. It lay
drugged into silence, one
poor cry would start a tyranny
of scimitars to run
the water red.

The fortunate
all have a tale to tell,
a million more remain untold.
Man has invented hell
searching for heaven.
                I have seen
the record of a face
on yellowed paper. Each bright day
obliterates the trace
this dead man left on space but cannot
dissipate his mind.
He wrote: "Why do we search for truth
as if we were born blind
or all existence were a lie?"
He knew the City. In
his day it still seemed possible
to find some way to win
it back. (The princess in her tower,
waiting the magic kiss.)
The vision was Byzantine with
the lost metropolis
the keystone to the arch of Empire,
the last citadel
to halt the barbarous assault.
Since then the infidel
has sprung among us. We have sewn
the dragons' teeth and fought
the monstrous crop.
                The City is
the womb to which our thought
regressed, but, lately, we have come
of age. We have returned
our trust to that far older city

19

where we first discerned
the quality of light. The temple
to the Goddess fords
the sky and all the growing buildings
orientate towards
those culminating columns. We
remember now our source
but cherish still the Church of Holy
Wisdom and the course
She set us. What we are we owe
to these two cities. We
have built upon their hearthstones, heirs
in perpetuity.

Augurs

The ancients read the flights of birds
for augurs. They observed
duck skeined across the moon and reckoned
up. This sum deserved
success but seldom turned out well.
Or they computed by
a watch of nightingales and made
predictions, or a sky
incised with swallows. They compiled
statistics from a string
of sparrows, made hypotenuse
out of an eagle's wing
and fixed the future from a charm
of goldfinch. Their design
was lovely and precise but they
neglected to define
the unknown quantity. If X
denotes the mind of man
no galaxy of wings nor bird-
starred constellations can
divine his course. Grant me my lark
ascending or concede
my throated thrush and I will tell
tomorrow's weather. Read
the heart's biometry and find
that two and two make five.
The birds are driven by their needs,
the first, to keep alive
and then to make their feathered love
and sing. But man creates
new appetites out of the leavings
of desire. He waits

for no just equinox to drive
him forward. He has made
his mark on fate but cannot pardon
what he has betrayed.

Propagation

Plato, in search of Justice,
had to postulate
a State, yet failed to flush
his quarry. Set the bait
and land a gaping boot,
or pull a rose apart,
to learn the source of beauty,
bare it to the heart
and boast of clammy rags.
Analysis will give
the odds and ends of truth,
the grave's prerogative —
cracked bones and teeth, perhaps
a fungoid growth of hair,
the verdigris on bronze,
the broken shards that share
death's privacy; with luck,
a mask of beaten gold
or amber ring to prove
that goods were bought and sold
from north to south. And such
sad sediment of fact
must serve to resurrect
the wellspring of the act.
That Roman citizen
and former Rabbi, Paul,
dissected Christianity
and built a wall
to heaven with the bits.
Whereas his Master spoke
of sparrows and likened Solomon
to lilies.

Stoke
what fire you can until
you burn that sparks may fly
out of the quickening ash
to kindle earth and sky.

Another Paradise

Neo-Byzantine churches
spring from Tessa's paint
brush, stuck with crosses like
an apple with cloves. Restraint
is not the keynote of
her style. Her eye translates
the symbols of a world
of beauty and creates
another paradise.
Four coloured domes cavort
across the paper, each
one splashed with windows. Swart
and elongate, a priest
appears inside a crimson
door. He pulls a rope
and it is up to him —
one sees this by the angle
of his beard — to keep
the bells upended in
their tower. The bells both leap
to hurdle heaven and
with tongues hung out they tell
perpetual music to
the stars. For these, as well
as sun and moon, emblazon
Tessa's scene. She shows
no servitude to time
but paints what is. She knows
the sky is crammed with gold
and spends the currency
to pay the debt in kind,
bequeathing joy to me.

25

She also paints her school
set in its garden where
the children grow like flowers.
She gives them coloured hair
and leafy arms. Like flowers
they show no sex. They climb
the lemon tree and sit
astride the roof. And time
again capitulates
to Tessa's will. The sun,
on golden tentacles,
crawls up the sky and one
redhanded child has caught
the moon.
           So Tessa paints
the Church and State in
microcosm and acquaints
me with their essence. Flowers
and bells and planets are
this cosmic company.
The children in the garden
turn their faces to
the sun and learn to see.

I like her views on art.
She has not come to be
intimidated by
her subject nor technique.
Her range is passionate
but then, she sees in Greek.

Time Harvested

I watch my daughter run
between the orange trees
and pick the glowing fruits
where they have fallen. These
she tumbles in my lap
prodigiously — a king,
with less munificence,
would fling his jewelled ring
to please a dancing girl.

This child, Teresa, chose
her treasure unremarked
by others, free for those
who see to gather up.
The child is innocent.
She puts no flaming sword
between her heart's intent
and Eden, and I watch
her run among the trees
and wait. If I am patient
she will find the keys
that I have lost and let
me in her kingdom where
the trumpet sounds, the sun
and moon bow down, the heir
assumes dominion.
                    I,
perhaps, presume too much.
I must discover my
own country and I touch
its frontiers now. I need
not travel further than

the eye can compass nor
exceed a moment's span.
In now I am contained
and void the future's threat,
the past a dream.
                    I wait,
then, where my heart is set,
amongst the orange trees
that grow in Greece, and tell
Teresa how I found
that other fruit which fell
in English orchards once.
The action has not changed.
The shapes of yesterday
are merely rearranged
to form today. As now,
both nourished by one root
the April orange blossom
springs amongst its fruit.

My daughter

I try to fix the face
of this beloved child
deep in my mind — a swan,
trapped in the ice and wild
to fly, or else a rose
held under water in
a globe of glass. My gaze
cannot suffice to win
me her image. I
pursue the tender zone
from cheek to brow; the eye
set in the hollowed bone
like topaz clawed in gold;
the petalled ear; the mouth,
sweet calyx of a flower, and still,
like one who suffers drouth,
spreadeagled in the sand,
powerless to gain the land
running with milk and honey,
my perceptions stand
outside the beaten door
of memory. I close
my eyes and on the lidded
dark seek to compose
her likeness. Were I blind
I could contain her form
with nearer truth, for she,
still centre of the storm,
remains inviolate.
Grant me a painter's eye
I might attempt to brush
her beauty onto my

recording brain, but, even
then I would possess
a shadow of what is.
No! nor her loveliness
is she. She would exist
a paragon to me
in other guise. Make dark
the fair and ivory
the pearl and I would find
perfection in her face.
For what I see and love
is not the carapace
my turtle turns to me,
this too, yet far beyond,
it is the stone that starts
the ripples on the pond.

Growth

My children grow
and I progress
more slowly than
their consciousness.
Their minds, like nets,
sweep up the seas,
catching them pearls
and ambergris,
while I throw back
the greedy fish
that take the worm
against my wish.
Perhaps I made
a better haul
when both my boasts
and bones were small.
Now I demand
my due and get
just that, or else
run into debt.
But children do
not make a sum
of what they rate
in kingdom come,
they enter, with
no backward glance,
into their full
inheritance.
I only need
their lack of doubt
to turn my losses
inside out

and, ignorant
of hope and dread,
upon the waters
cast my bread.

Parents observed

The acorn falls. The tree,
rooted in solid clay,
appears as if all growth must be
towards decay.
The child perceives the man
cast in a final mould
and thinks he no more changes than
a toy grown old.
Imaged in these eyes
and startled out of youth
I understand my own surprise
finding the truth
that parents are not set
stubbornly in stone
but slough their skins like snakes and get
nearer the bone.
Lovers caught up by age,
vulnerable, unplanned —
I see my parents at the stage
where I now stand.

Middle age

And suddenly one finds
one's unsuspecting face
is forty if a day,
just when it knows its place
and can be counted on
to varnish the plain truth
one cries for that clear moon
that lit one's awkward youth.

The Old Woman

This old woman's memory,
they say, is failing. She forgets
where she has laid her glasses or
the grocer's bill. The household frets
to find the trivia she puts
from her — they do not understand
she has no need to tie herself
to life with things.
                          Give her your hand
and this she recognizes, she
accepts the claim of flesh and blood
to hold her here. And yet, she waits,
the whole of life has come to bud
in now. She feels the tender force
which pulls her petals open and
she knows that when she breaks in flower
she breaks with all the past. No hand
will keep that springing rose from bloom.

They say her memory is weak.
She does not care to stamp her mind
with modern currency and seek
to bargain with today. Her gold
was minted long ago and bears
the heads of kings. Nor does she wish
discourtesy but though she hears
their importunate voices she
must hold to her intent and let
the silence spin about her. Time
has lost its tyranny — forget?
Ah no, remember. In her lap
her yesterdays all lie. This final
task awaits her. She must sort
each finished piece and put it by.

Love Poem

Assure me only this,
that when you hurl your rage
at my obdurate head
it is not to assuage
your demon. I require
to know which one of us
you hate — myself or that
despotic incubus
to whom you grant asylum.
I can bear the beast
that claws my eyes in fear,
the vulture at its feast
of greed upon my heart,
this savagery is pure,
I am its object and
I shudder but endure.
But if I am the thing
on which you retch your guilt,
the sacrifice interred
before the tower is built,
if I am used to lay
your ghost, I die.
      Assure
me yet again that when
you take my mouth in your
consuming kiss, you take
me as I am. I can
not match the dream you wish
on me, the perfect plan
of what I ought to be.

It seems that love's first strike

of recognition shows
us in our essence like
the arrow which impales
an apple to its core.
The usages of love
corrupt. We meet no more
as entities but make
in one another's stead
an effigy to stuff
in a Procrustean bed,
and should we bark out shins
on truth we mutilate
its form that it may fit.

It still is not too late
my love — oh be my love
and let us learn our true
identity. We must
return to that first view
which gave us each to each.
The body is a chart,
it is one way to reach
the country of the heart.
I put my roots into
your soil and grow, so let
me be and you enroot
yourself in me. Thickset
we'll put forth leaves and make
a place for birds to sing.
Accept my head to lie
beside your own and bring
your centre here to rest.
Enclose with yours my mouth

and nightingales will fly
to our magnetic south.

The solipsism

We lie our bodies down
and seek with practised hands
that solipsism, sex,
where each one understands
the other's need but shares
only the means. The end
takes place in common time
but what we apprehend
is separate.
         The blood
drums in the symphony
of sense, the body climbs
the clonic scale and we,
on one sweet bugle note,
ride out the singing tide.
We only know one personal
event and hide
our lonely ecstasy
in mutual gratitude.
"My love," we say, "my love."
And cover up the nude,
exploited form of truth.
"My love," we say, and try
to love but cannot get
away from me and my.

The spear

He scratches lines on rock
aped by his shadow. Beasts
lurch under that hand,
precursor of all priests
invoking Heaven. He,
prey to the sabretooth
and wolf, has mastered fire.
Squat, hairy and uncouth
he works in light to make
ochre and charcoal bind
an antelope to stone.
So, in the hunters' mind
tomorrow's meat takes shape.
This is to pray. The Greeks
and Jews, no longer
innocent, employed techniques,
libations, sacrifice
and ceremonies, aimed
to pleasure God. The rot
had started, man defamed
his own idea of truth.
Prayer cannot buttonhole
Divinity nor jolt
an arm but knows the sole
reality is lived
in God, the biosphere.
Imagine, then, an
antelope and raise the spear.

The Naked Ape

Poor, naked ape!
His nature welded by
a chain of accidents;
his genes prepackaged; shape
as specified; dye
fast to its elements;
health an inheritance
invested by trustees.
Wean him too soon, too late;
pot him or not; the chance
choice between chalk or cheese,
the gamble of love or hate
all dished up like a meal
he has to eat — or get
it cold for supper. He
is bound upon a wheel
he once called Fate and yet
his cry of agony
must wait upon events.
Still naked, he has formed,
with time, a carapace
scratched with the ornaments
of learning. He has warmed
his bones in the embrace
of beauty and has found
the weapon of the mind
sharper than teeth or claws.
What next? He holds his ground
but cannot be resigned
to marking time. The laws
of man and jungle fail
to satisfy some itch

he suckled on — the old
Adam and the tale
told in a garden which
blows him first hot then cold.
Poor, hopeful clown!
He had to invent a God
to walk with in the shade
and cannot live it down.
His hairy cousins trod
the treetops and displayed
their monkey tricks while he,
biting a horny nail,
must dream up angels, powers
and principality.
At least he shed a tail
during those brooding hours
and gave to things a name.
And now he's stuck right there,
a spectre at the feast
with only himself to blame.
But where to go from here?
Poor, battered beast!

But one thing is needful

By any lights she was
a virtuous woman. She
embraced her duty like
a husband and could be
as jealous for her home
as for a man. Each night
before she slept her thoughts
inspected with delight
the ordered day. No girl
could bring to mind the glance
and glitter of her lover
in a sweeter trance
than she. A task undone
would call her like a fretful
child. She could not sleep
unless she rose and set
the thing to right.
        She kept
the Sabbath — but her hands
picked at such idleness.
Twisting her turquoise bands
up to the stubborn knuckle
she would brood. And burn
to tread her loom or make
the creaking spindle turn
and pull the savage wool
into a tempered thread.
She paid her proper dues —
but finished in her head
taut lengths of cloth and then
measured and stitched and broke
the phantom yarn and dreamed

her brother's winter cloak.

She loved the changing year;
each season brought its own
demands for her to meet.
She loved each stick and stone
that made her home. She loved
the pots, the earthenware,
the copper pans, the jars
of flour and oil. Her care
was like a blessing, what
she wrought she lifted up
to its own excellence.
A wooden spoon, a cup,
a bowl set on the table
made a masterpiece.

She knew what loving meant
and, working without cease,
she loved. She loved her brother
though his entity
was fluid, she could not
confine him, could not see
his final form nor mould
the shape to which he grew.
She loved her sister but
with her she strove. She knew
what woman was and what
her flower should be, and did
not understand this alien
blossoming. But hid
these thoughts and cherished all
under her careful hand.

And then, he came, her brother's
friend, and she would stand
stockstill from happiness.
His words were like the stone
and timber of her house,
each syllable was known
to her and yet built up
the perfect dwelling place.
And other friends would come,
crowding the little space,
her brother bringing each
one in as to a feast.
She listened — then would start
up like a goaded beast
to do the honours of
the house, fetching a chair
or pulling out a chest
to make a seat. Aware
again, recalled to self,
ready to use her skill,
a meal to cook, the best
she could provide, her will
to work on things. She had
to bake new bread and get
cold water from the well,
unlock her linen, set
the table, pour the wine . . .

And with no thought at all
her sister sat at Jesus' feet
and let her petals fall.

Here is a cold country.
I walk on stone beside
this English chief, wrapped
to the chin, and watch the tide
of his grey river bear
strange traffic to the sea.
We stamp and turn.
Barren
of flowers or fruit a tree
shivers and drips its leaves
and we, shivering, light
tobacco and breathe sweet spice
and fire. The sky is white
with cold and cold the stone.
Towers rise and walls
built by a cold people.
No God lives here. The halls
are bare of gold. They raise
stone upon stone to shun
hot-hearted men like he.
Dishonoured the sun.

Cruelty and hate
I know, these are the face
of fear. I do not know
indifference. Disgrace
is death and carelessness
is death. To kill the snake
before it strikes, to spear
the jungle cat, to take
life like a man to live.
And, treachery to kill,

46

to let the whoring blood
out at the throat until
corruption cannot claim
our brotherhood. Death
is the decision of a chief
but here the breath
bears no authority.
It seems I learn new things,
the ship that brought me over
seas has clapped its wings
and fled. Where are my sparkling
birds? I walk on stone
beside my friend and devils
ride the air, blown
on the wind, grey, black and white,
thirsty for blood. At home
the birds sip honey, wings
flickering flowers, and comb
the heavy air with streaks
of light. The water slides,
green into green, and trees
offer fruit like brides.

Here is a new world. I,
a chief, must stay unknown,
outcast to Northern eyes,
a forest bird blown
out to sea. And he? My mind
fills up, I understand.
I see an eagle broken
winged, lurching on land
while creatures who once ran
in terror now grow bold
and wait to watch him die.

I walk beside this old
caged eagle and
I see a man who makes
all worlds his own, a rich
discoverer who takes
the gift of life and pours
out gold to everyone.
We call such men: Beloved —
Eagles of the Sun.